D1395121

The Story of Pirates

Rob Lloyd Jones

Illustrated by Vincent Dutrait

History consultant: Richard Platt
Reading consultant: Alison Kelly, Roehampton University

Contents

Chapter 1

Ancient pirates

Over 2,000 years ago, pirates roamed the seas. Gangs of bloodthirsty seafarers scoured the coasts of the Roman empire, hunting for merchant ships carrying valuable cargos of silver, olive oil or grain. When they spotted one, they followed it out to sea, waiting for the moment to attack.

Racing swiftly over the waves in ships known as galleys, the pirates bore down on their target. Rows of oarsmen heaved back and forth, powering the ships along. Other pirates cheered ferociously, waving swords still encrusted with blood from previous battles.

A ten-foot bronze ram extended from the front of their galley, crowned with spikes. It was aimed directly at the side of the merchant ship.

Crashing into the ship, the ram shattered open the vessel's side. The merchant sailors watched in horror, as pirates swarmed on board with wild battle cries. The pirates had captured their prize.

Over 600 years later, during the 8th century, pirates from Scandinavia, known as Vikings, terrorized European waters. The Vikings sailed in flat-bottomed vessels called longships, designed to be rowed right up onto the beach.

Then they stormed inland, looting houses, shops, and even churches and monasteries. They also captured thousands of men, women and children to be sold as slaves back home.

By the 15th century, pirates called corsairs sailed the Mediterranean Sea. They were involved in a religious war between Christians and Muslims. Christian corsairs attacked Muslim ships, and Muslim corsairs plundered Christian vessels. They fought for their religion, but kept whatever treasures they found on board for themselves.

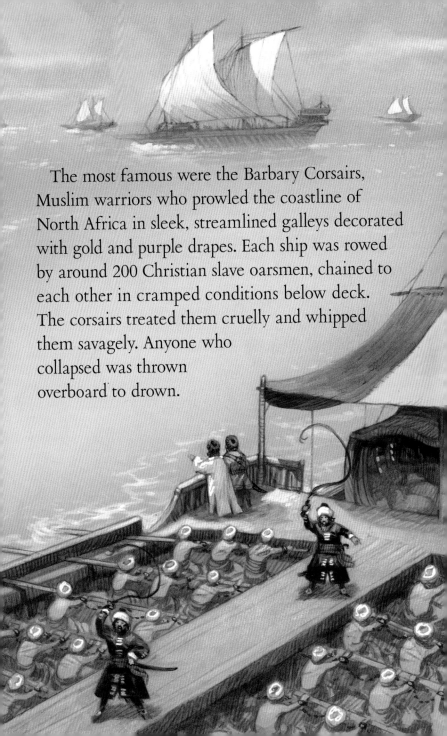

The most famous were the Barbary Corsairs, Muslim warriors who prowled the coastline of North Africa in sleek, streamlined galleys decorated with gold and purple drapes. Each ship was rowed by around 200 Christian slave oarsmen, chained to each other in cramped conditions below deck. The corsairs treated them cruelly and whipped them savagely. Anyone who collapsed was thrown overboard to drown.

Perhaps the most terrifying of them were Aruj and Khei-ed-Din, known as the Barbarossa (which meant 'red-beard') brothers. The Barbarossas commanded a huge fleet of galleys that attacked Dutch and English ships throughout the Mediterranean. Storming on board brandishing curved swords known as scimitars, their savage appearance often terrified victims into instant surrender.

By the 17th century, Holland and England had built strong navies to protect their trading ships. So the corsairs were no longer such a threat.

But on the other side of the world, new groups of pirates had begun to wreak havoc on merchant ships in the Caribbean Sea. The Golden Age of piracy had begun.

Chapter 2

The Golden Age

In the 17th century, the town of Port Royal, in Jamaica, was a bustling hive of activity. Dozens of ships sat at anchor, creating a forest of masts and rigging. Rows of timber houses lined the docks, merchants loaded crates onto their ships, fishermen untangled nets, and horses pulled carts over the cobbled streets.

Lurking among them were pirates.

The tropical sea around Jamaica was the ideal hunting ground for pirates. Ever since Spanish explorers had discovered America almost 200 years earlier, the Spanish government had mined vast quantities of silver and gold, as well as precious jewels, from Peru, Mexico and Colombia.

Chests of the treasure were loaded onto Spanish warships, known as galleons, and sailed back to Europe. The ships always followed the same route through the Caribbean Sea, passing Colombia, Panama, Mexico, and then onto Cuba – an area known as the Spanish Main. By the 17th century, wealthy ports such as Port Royal were dotted all over the coasts.

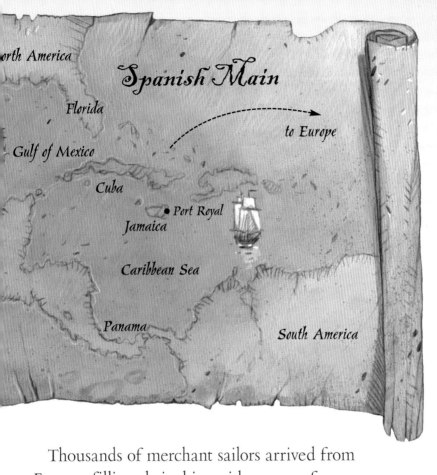

Spanish Main

North America

Florida

Gulf of Mexico

Cuba

Port Royal

Jamaica

Caribbean Sea

Panama

South America

to Europe

Thousands of merchant sailors arrived from Europe, filling their ships with cargos of sugar, exotic spices and luxury cloth to sell back home. It wasn't long before they were targeted by some of the most famous pirates in history.

Over the previous hundred years, England and Spain had been at war. The English queen, Elizabeth I, gave many English captains documents, known as letters of marque, which allowed them to attack ships belonging to her enemies. The captains could keep a share of whatever treasures they stole.

These sailors who stole from their enemies were known as privateers. One of the most successful was Sir Francis Drake. From 1577 to 1580, he sailed around the world in his ship the *Golden Hinde*. Along the way, he plundered vast amounts of gold from Spanish warships.

On his return to England, the Queen came aboard Drake's ship and rewarded him with a knighthood.

A privateer's letters of marque, though, could only be used during wartime. After the wars finished, many privateers carried on attacking ships, including those from their own country. From then on, they were pirates.

Any crew members who disagreed were replaced at the next port. Pirate captains often recruited new crew members in dingy taverns, buying them drinks and telling them tales of great fortunes to be made. Usually, they chose hardened seafarers who had already served on navy or merchant ships for little pay. To them, the lure of treasure was irresistible.

Becoming a pirate was called going on account. Each pirate signed a document agreeing to the rules he would live by on the pirate ship. These rules, known as the pirate code, were often much fairer than those on strict merchant or navy ships. But they also reminded the pirates of their duties:

All treasure will be shared out equally among the pirates, except for the captain, who gets double.

All pirates may vote on important decisions.

Any pirate who is lazy or fails to clean his weapons will be whipped.

Any pirates who run away during battle will be caught and killed.

Once the sailors had agreed to the pirate code, they followed the captain through the docks to their new home – the pirate ship.

In the Golden Age, most pirates sailed on ships known as sloops. These were shallow vessels that were ideal for launching quick attacks on enemy ships or hiding out in secluded bays. But they were often very small, with as many as a hundred pirates living on board. Pirates could sail for weeks before they found a merchant ship to attack. So conditions quickly became cramped and uncomfortable.

Pirate ships were crammed with all sorts of provisions – ropes, spare sails, grimy anchor cable, crates of food, and barrels of beer and water. There were often animals on board, too: hens in cages, goats in pens, even cows if there was room. Each animal created its own mess, adding to the general filth on board.

Most of the time, pirates kept themselves busy with the day-to-day duties of sailing. Some of them had their own special jobs. The gunner repaired and cleaned the ship's cannons, for instance, and the sailing master was in charge of navigating the vessel. But other pirates had more basic duties, such as hauling ropes or scrubbing the decks.

Every few months, the pirates had to clean the bottom, or hull, of their ship. After a while at sea, it would be covered in barnacles, seaweed, and tiny toredo worms, which ate through the wood and caused leaks that could sink the ship if they weren't fixed.

To repair and clean the hull, pirates sailed
their ship into a secluded bay. Then, when the
tide went out, they heaved it over on one side
using ropes and pulleys. Then they fixed any
leaks by stuffing them with old rope and
covering them in a thick layer of
sticky tar. This job was called
careening. It was hot, thirsty
work, and could take as
long as two weeks.

Careening gave pirates an opportunity to collect more food and water. But, even so, supplies still didn't last long. Early on a pirate voyage, the crew ate a varied diet that included fish, turtle, grapes and eggs. To drink, they carried barrels of rum, beer and water. But the water quickly ran out, and food rotted in the tropical heat. Soon, the only food left was a kind of hard biscuit known as tack. These became so infested with insects that pirates could only stomach eating them in the dark.

They would try to raise their spirits by singing or telling stories, but frustration boiled over, and fights often broke out on board.

The pirate captain knew that if he failed to find a ship to attack soon, his crew might mutiny, turning against their captain and replacing him with someone else.

But they couldn't just attack any ship they spotted. The captain needed to be sure of two things: first, that the ship was weaker than his and could be defeated in battle, and second, that it carried enough treasure to make an attack worthwhile. Sometimes, pirates followed a potential victim for days, watching them load new cargos at different ports.

Often the pirate captain discussed the situation with the ship's quartermaster, who was the second in command. Once he had made his decision, he gave the order. "Prepare your weapons," he shouted to his crew. "Attack!"

Chapter 3

Attack!

Moments before an attack, the deck of a pirate ship swarmed with activity. The crew adjusted the sails, loaded cannons, and prepared weapons – cutlass swords, daggers, and flintlock pistols. Some of the pirates hung two or three pistols on strings around their necks, in case one of them jammed or became wet with sea spray. High above, at the top of the main mast, flew the famous pirate flag – the *Jolly Roger*.

The *Jolly Roger* was one of the most terrifying sights a merchant sailor could see. The flag's name is thought to have come from the pirates' nickname for the devil, *Old Roger*. Pirates hoped it would strike fear into the hearts of their enemies, causing instant surrender.

The most common version of the flag showed a skull with two crossed bones, but many pirate captains adapted it in their own style, with skull and crossed swords, or more sinister symbols such as skeletons, or hearts dripping with blood.

The sign sailors feared most, though, was the red pirate flag – a warning that no mercy would be shown in battle.

Merchant sailors could only watch in horror as pirates approached. Their ships were usually too slow to outrun them, or facing the wrong direction to fire their cannons at them. They had few other weapons on board to defend themselves with, and no means of calling for help. Their best chance of survival was to offer the pirates instant surrender. But they knew they might be killed anyway.

Suddenly, the pirates would be upon them. The pirate ship crashed against the merchant vessel, running itself alongside. Some of the pirates jammed wooden wedges into the merchant ship's rudder to stop it from steering away, while others tied hooks to the ends of ropes, known as grappling hooks, and hurled them into the rigging. Heaving the ropes, they pulled the two ships together and, with savage yells, leaped onto the merchant ship's deck.

The next few minutes of a pirate attack would be chaotic. Hungry for treasure, the pirates ransacked the ship, tearing open hatches, emptying cupboards and smashing crates. Any sailors who resisted were killed instantly and thrown to the sharks. The others were tied up and held captive in the middle of the deck.

Some pirates found valuable Spanish coins such as silver 'pieces of eight' or gold 'doubloons', but most simply grabbed anything they could sell back on land – spices, luxury cloth, or even just spare sails and old rope. All of this would be divided among the pirate crew, according to the pirate code.

After they had looted everything they could sell, the pirates stole any food and drink on board, as well as any weapons they might be able to use in future attacks. Sometimes they even stole the ship itself – but not often. Pirates usually preferred sailing their own speedy sloops to the larger, slower merchant vessels.

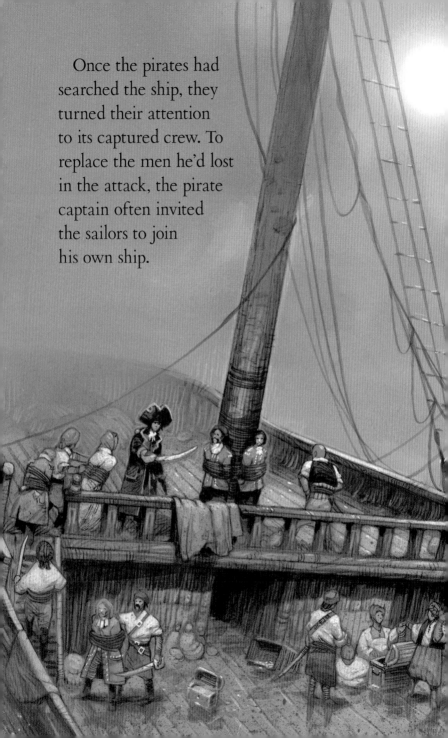

Once the pirates had searched the ship, they turned their attention to its captured crew. To replace the men he'd lost in the attack, the pirate captain often invited the sailors to join his own ship.

Many accepted, happy to leave behind their hard lives under the merchant captain. Others, though, were made to join. These were skilled men, such as carpenters or surgeons, who were needed on board the pirates' ship.

Often, the pirates left their victims shaken but unharmed. But some merchant crews faced a more grisly fate – torture. Sometimes pirates tortured captives for fun, but usually they did it to discover where they had hidden their treasure, using beatings, mutilations, or other horrible forms of violence.

One woman who refused to hand over her jewels was shoved into a barrel of gunpowder, which the pirates threatened to light. She quickly gave up her treasure, and the pirates set her free.

Perhaps the worst fate that a victim of a pirate attack could suffer, though, was to be left to die on a desert island, a punishment known as marooning. While some desert islands had fresh water and shade from the sun, most were simply empty sandbanks in the sea. Anyone left on one had little hope of being spotted or rescued by a passing ship. Instead, they faced a slow, agonizing death from dehydration or sunstroke. Usually, pirates left marooners with a pistol and a single bullet – to use on themselves.

But marooning
wasn't reserved for the
victims of pirate attacks.
Pirates who broke the
pirate code or attempted mutiny
often suffered the same terrible
fate. Some pirate captains even
marooned members of their own
crew, just so there would be
fewer left to share the treasure.

Even though pirates were cruel to their victims, they could be kind to each other. Pirates who were injured in battle usually received an extra share of the treasure to compensate. Some pirate codes spelled out exactly how much they should get.

Compensation for injury in pieces of eight

Loss of eye: 100

Loss of finger: 100

Loss of right arm: 600

Loss of left arm: 500

Loss of right leg: 500

Loss of left leg: 400

Most injured pirates took
their money ashore at the next port,
where they quickly spent it on drink
and gambling. Others continued sailing
with the pirates, doing whatever jobs
they could. A pirate who lost a leg
often became the ship's cook, toiling
over a stove as his shipmates set off
in search of fresh victims.

Chapter 4

Cruel captains

While most pirates were lawless and uneducated, their captains were often intelligent, calculating characters. Each one led a crew of violent criminals, who would happily turn against him in a mutiny if they weren't capturing enough treasure.

Different captains used different ways to keep control. Some earned their respect through success in battle. Others demanded it through fear.

One of the most frightening pirate captains was Francois l'Ollonais, a French pirate who terrorized the Spanish Main in the 17th century. After capturing a ship, l'Ollonais treated its crew with savage brutality. He sliced their flesh from their arms, set them on fire, and much worse.

Even so, l'Ollonais's fearsome reputation rarely made his enemies surrender. They knew he would kill them anyway, so fighting back was their only chance.

Almost fifty years later, a pirate captain with an even more terrifying image sailed the Spanish Main – Edward Teach, better known as Blackbeard. Blackbeard was a huge man, with a thick, tangled beard, and teeth that were little more than rotten stumps. Anyone who saw him in battle swore he was the devil. Before each attack, he twisted lengths of fuse into his hair and set them alight. Then he charged into battle engulfed in a cloud of smoke.

Unlike Francois l'Ollonais, though, Blackbeard rarely harmed his victims. Instead, he used his savage appearance to force them to surrender. Those who didn't regretted it quickly. One merchant refused to hand Blackbeard a ring he was wearing, so the captain simply slashed the man's hand off and took it himself.

Blackbeard also used his savage reputation to keep control of his crew. Once, while he and a crewmate were drinking on board his ship, the *Queen Anne's Revenge*, Blackbeard simply shot the man without warning. The rest of the crew demanded to know their captain's motive, but Blackbeard just grinned. "If I don't kill one of you now and again," he said, "you might forget who I am."

While Blackbeard earned his crew's respect, another famous pirate captain, Stede Bonnet, paid for it. Before becoming a pirate, the polite Englishman lived comfortably with his wife on the island of Barbados. He had a large house, many friends, and was well regarded among the island's high society.

Then, sometime in 1717, he just decided to become a pirate. No one knows why. He had no knowledge of the sea, and certainly none of piracy. Rather than stealing a ship, like most pirates did, Bonnet bought one for himself. Then he rounded up 70 vagabond sailors from the island, and paid them to become his pirate crew.

The sailors were happy to accept Bonnet's money. They guided his ship along the east coast of America, attacking merchant vessels at his command. Soon, though, they realized their captain had little idea what he was doing. All day, Bonnet paraded around the deck dressed in expensive clothes, well-polished shoes and a fancy wig.

Then, one day in 1718, they sailed into the Bay of Honduras and their ship came face-to-face with one belonging to a real pirate – Blackbeard.

Blackbeard recognized Bonnet as an amateur almost immediately. Even so, he invited the fancily dressed captain on board and treated him to a night of feasting and drinking.

Bonnet was flattered by Blackbeard's friendship. He stayed on the *Queen Anne's Revenge* for six months, happily lounging about reading books in his dressing gown, while Blackbeard's crew commanded his own ship.

But, when Bonnet finally returned to his ship, he found it stripped bare. Blackbeard had stolen all of his treasure – as well as most of his crew.

Undeterred, Bonnet gathered a new crew and continued as a pirate until September, when he was captured by the British Royal Navy off the coast of North Carolina, in North America. While awaiting trial, Bonnet wrote a letter appealing to the state governor.

"Please," he begged, "whatever you do, please don't hang me!"

But the governor had no pity. Bonnet was hanged as a pirate on December 10, 1718.

Blackbeard died the same year, but in very different circumstances. Sailing along the coast of North Carolina, the *Queen Anne's Revenge* was attacked by two Royal Navy ships, carrying sixty men. After a furious cannon fight, Blackbeard crashed his ship alongside one of the navy vessels and stormed on board, screaming and swinging his swords.

The British sailors fired several times, but the pirate kept charging, killing several of them before finally falling himself. When they examined Blackbeard's body, they discovered it had taken five bullets and twenty cutlass blows to kill him. They cut off his head and hung the grisly trophy from the front of their ship, proud to have defeated the most notorious pirate in the Spanish Main.

Chapter 5

Pirates defeated

Dark clouds rumbled over the west coast of
Africa on February 10, 1722, as the *Royal
Fortune* raced through the driving rain. On its deck,
the famous pirate captain Bartholomew Roberts
looked back at the ship that was chasing them. It
was a British warship, heavily armed and flying the
flag of King George.

Roberts watched the warship drawing closer with the trace of a smile on his face. He knew he was about to be caught, but he didn't mind. His motto had always been *"A merry life, and a short one"* – and his had been very merry indeed. Over the past four years, he had plundered more than 400 ships, from the Spanish Main to the Red Sea.

But, with merchant ships under such constant attack, the British government had finally decided to fight back. The Royal Navy had begun to hunt for pirates in powerful ships called men-of-war, armed with as many as 120 guns. Small pirate sloops had no chance against such vessels.

Even so, Roberts was determined to go down fighting.

He pulled on his finest crimson waistcoat, flamboyant feathered hat, and hung a priceless diamond cross around his neck on a gold chain. Then, slinging a pair of pistols on a belt over his shoulder, he shouted for his crew to prepare for battle.

Suddenly, the navy ship began firing. Cannon blasts tore through the *Royal Fortune*, sending deadly splinters flying everywhere. As the smoke cleared, Captain Bartholomew Roberts lay dead on the deck.

The defeat of Bartholomew Roberts was a huge triumph in the Royal Navy's war against pirates. The year before, King George had announced that any pirate who surrendered would receive an official pardon. This excused them of their crimes, as long as they swore not to commit any more in the future.

Many pirates were happy to accept the offer. The royal pardon gave them an opportunity to take whatever money they had left and retire to a new life. Others, though, swore to continue to the death. In response, the British government sent even more ships to fight them.

Led by ambitious young captains, these warships spent months hunting down pirates and defeating them in dramatic sea battles. Those who were caught alive faced trial for piracy and murder. Those who were found guilty were hung.

Between 1716 and 1726, more than 400 men were executed for piracy. Some of the hangings took place in towns along the east coast of America, or in Caribbean ports such as Port Royal. Other pirates were taken back to England in chains, where they were executed in front of huge crowds.

The most famous pirate to be hung in London was the English captain William Kidd. Like many pirates, Kidd had begun his career as a privateer, before turning to piracy in 1698. Sailing in his ship the *Adventure Galley*, he attacked vessels from the Caribbean to the Indian Ocean, before his capture a year later in Boston, North America.

Kidd's death was typical of many pirates of the Golden Age. After almost a year locked in a dark, dank prison cell with little food or water, he was clamped in chains and carried in a cart to Execution Dock – a site beside the River Thames where all pirates were hung.

Huge crowds gathered for pirate executions, roaring with delight as the pirate swore and spat at them from the back of the cart. By now, he was usually so drunk he had to be carried up a ladder onto the gallows, as the hangman slipped a noose around his neck. Then he was pushed from the ladder to hang.

Any friends in the crowd would rush forward, pulling his legs from below to quicken his death. When William Kidd was executed, though, the rope snapped, and he had to be hanged all over again.

After his death, William Kidd's body was coated in thick tar and clamped in an iron cage, known as a gibbet chain. These cages hung beside the River Thames for as long as two years, a grisly warning to all sailors that the great age of piracy was over.

Chapter 6

Pirates: fact and fiction

The Golden Age of piracy ended almost 300 years ago, but pirates continue to terrorize the seas today. Although there are fewer of them nowadays, modern pirates still operate in the Caribbean, as well as in the waters around Southeast Asia and the South China Sea.

These eastern oceans have been popular with pirates for centuries. Just over a hundred years ago, they sailed in fleets of ships known as junks. The most powerful Chinese pirate captains commanded over 800 junks, and had as many as 70,000 pirates working for them. These vast pirate fleets surrounded merchant ships, forcing them into surrender. Those that refused were blown from the water.

Today's pirates operate in much smaller groups. Instead of sailing ships, they use speedboats to sneak onto ships at night.

But the most famous pirates remain those of the Golden Age. Many of the myths about these men come from modern movies and books that portray them as comedy characters, or even swashbuckling heroes.

Here, an actor plays Captain Hook in a theatrical production of *Peter Pan*. His comic appearance is typical of the way pirates are often portrayed in movies and plays.

The best-known pirate
story ever is probably
Treasure Island, written
in 1883 by Robert Louis
Stevenson. This story,
about a boy's adventures
with a gang of pirates
led by Long John Silver,
described the best-
known pirate pastime
of all – burying
treasure. But, in fact,
there's little evidence
that any pirate ever
actually did this. Most
of them preferred to
spend any treasure that they stole.

This illustration from a book of
pirate stories shows a pirate captain
watching while his crew buries
treasure on a beach. In fact, it's
unlikely that this ever happened.

Similarly, pirates didn't walk the plank, carry
parrots on their shoulders, or have hooked hands
and eye patches. Some of them did have wooden
legs, but not as many as you'd think from stories
such as *Treasure Island* or *Peter Pan*.

Real pirates drank a lot, cursed a lot, and killed
a lot. They weren't heroes at all – they were brutal
and bloodthirsty villains.

Other famous pirates and privateers

Sir Henry Morgan

Welsh privateer Henry Morgan led several daring
raids against Spanish ships and towns in the Spanish Main.
In 1669, he escaped the Spanish navy by loading one of his ships
with gunpowder, sailing it towards the enemy – and blowing it up.

Alexander Selkirk

In 1703, privateer William Dampier marooned Scottish seaman
Alexander Selkirk on an island off the coast of Chile. Selkirk lived
there alone for over four years, and his amazing story of survival
inspired the book *Robinson Crusoe* by Daniel Defoe.

Woodes Rogers

English privateer Woodes Rogers sailed around the world between
1708 and 1711, plundering Spanish ships. He later became one of
the most successful pirate hunters in history.

Samuel Bellamy

Bellamy's career as a pirate captain lasted less than a year, between
1716 and 1717, but he captured more than fifty ships. His kindness
to captives earned him the nickname *The Prince of Pirates*.

Anne Bonny and Mary Read

Pirates believed that having women on board ships brought bad
luck, so Anne Bonny and Mary Read had to disguise themselves as
men to join captain Jack Rackham's crew. Still, they were as skilled
at sea and brutal in battle as any of their shipmates.

Charles Vane

One of the most savage pirate captains of the Golden Age, Charles Vane was famous for his cruel treatment of captives. He even cheated his own crew, breaking the pirate code to take a bigger share of stolen loot for himself. His men finally mutinied against him in 1718. A year later, he was shipwrecked on an island off the Bay of Honduras.

Benjamin Hornigold

English captain Benjamin Hornigold wasn't quite as greedy as some other pirates. One story claims he captured a ship only to steal the crew's hats – his own men had thrown theirs overboard when they were drunk.

Henry Avery

In 1695, English captain Henry Avery attacked a ship on the Indian Ocean belonging to the ruler of India. He stole over half a million gold coins – one of the biggest treasure hauls in the history of piracy.

Bartholomew Portugues

Portuguese pirate Bartholomew Portugues was captured by the Spanish navy, but managed to escape by leaping overboard and swimming to safety. He quickly stole a new ship and continued his life as a pirate.

Madame Ching

Chinese pirate Madame Ching was one of the most successful pirates in history, leading a fleet of over 2,000 ships and more than 70,000 pirates. She was incredibly strict – any pirate who broke her pirate code risked having their ears, arms or head chopped off.

Designed by Andrea Slane
Edited by Jane Chisholm

First published in 2007 by Usborne Publishing Ltd,
Usborne House, 83-85 Saffron Hill, London EC1N 8RT, England.
www.usborne.com

Acknowledgements:
© ArenaPal/TopFoto p61; © Blue Lantern Studio/Corbis p60

Internet links

For links to websites where you can find out more about the lives
of famous pirates, go to the Usborne Quicklinks Website
at www.usborne-quicklinks.com and type the keywords Story of Pirates.
The recommended websites are regularly reviewed and updated but,
please note, Usborne Publishing is not responsible for the content of
websites other than its own.